Top College Football National Championship Games

BY RYAN JAMES

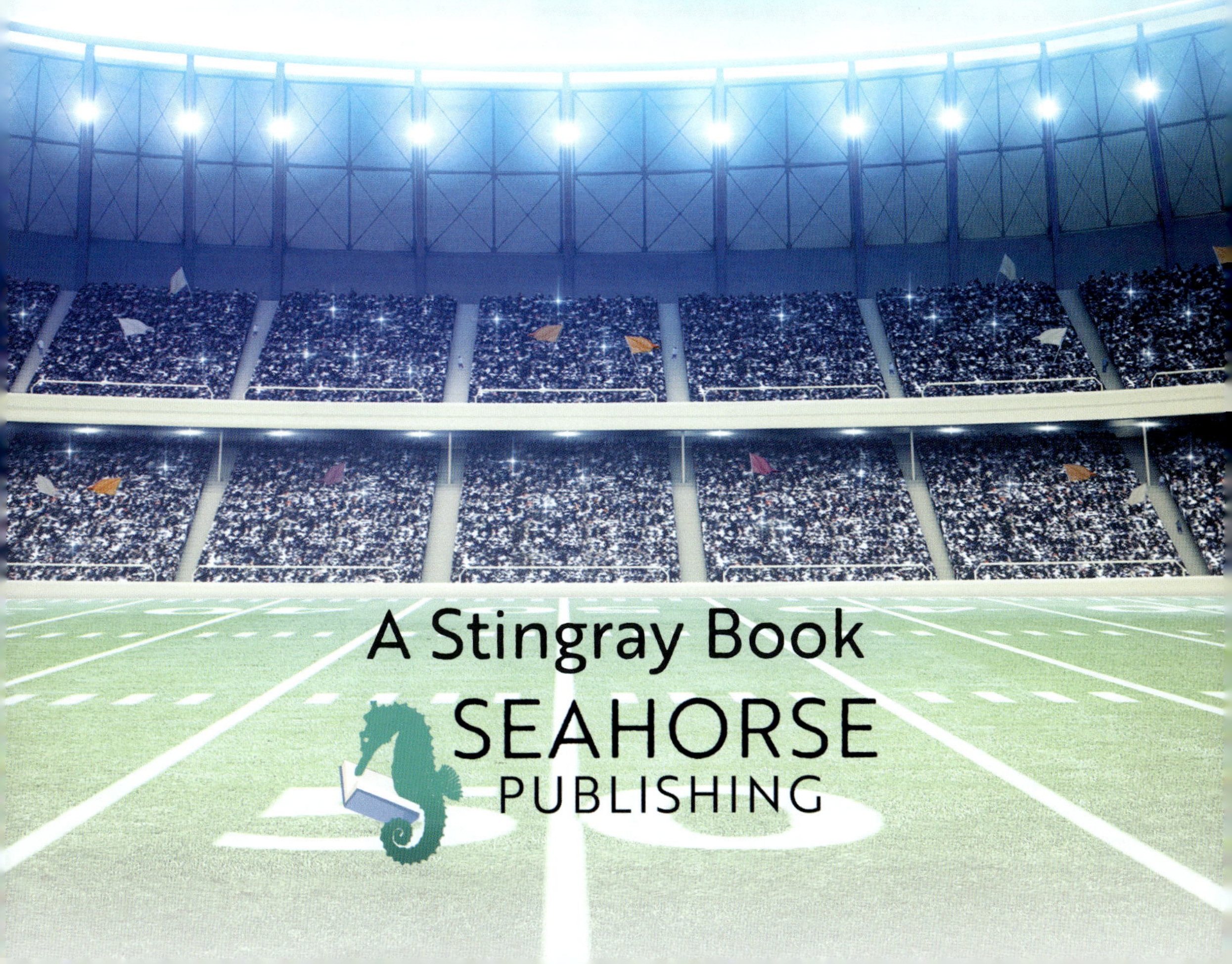

A Stingray Book

SEAHORSE
PUBLISHING

Teaching Tips for Caregivers and Teachers:

This Hi-Lo book features high-interest subject matter that will appeal to all readers in intermediate and middle school grades. It may be enjoyed by students reading at or above grade level as well as by those who are looking for age-appropriate themes matched with a less challenging reading level. Hi-Lo books are ideal for ELL readers, too.

Each book appeals to a striving reader's age and maturity level. Opportunities are provided for students to read words they already know while encountering a limited number of new, high-interest vocabulary words. With these supports in place, students will read more fluently while increasing reading comprehension. Use the following suggestions to help students grow as readers.

- Encourage the student to read independently at home.
- Encourage the student to practice reading aloud.
- Encourage activities that require reading.
- Establish a regular reading time.
- Have the student write questions about what they read.

Teaching Tips for Teachers:

Before Reading

- Ask, "What do I know about this topic?"
- Ask, "What do I want to learn about this topic?"

During Reading

- Ask, "What is the author trying to teach me?"
- Ask, "How is this like something I already know?"

After Reading

- Discuss how the text features (headings, index, etc.) help with understanding the topic.
- Ask, "What interesting or fun fact did you learn?"

TABLE OF CONTENTS

What Is the College Football National Championship Game?

The College Football National Championship Game is a football game that decides the best college team in the United States. It is played after the regular season ends.

The first championship game was played in 1883 between the Yale Bulldogs and the Harvard Crimson.

Today, the top four college teams are chosen by the College Football Playoff Selection Committee to compete in two **playoff** games. The winners of those games play in the national championship game.

FUN FACT: Yale University has won the most national championships with 18 victories.

YALE
33
3

2003 Tostitos Fiesta Bowl

January 3, 2003

OHIO STATE BUCKEYES 31-24 MIAMI HURRICANES

SUN DEVIL FOOTBALL STADIUM, TEMPE, ARIZONA

Miami kicker Todd Sievers kicked a 40-yard (36.5-meter) field goal at the end of the game for a tie. The game went into double **overtime**.

Ohio State **running back** Maurice Clarett scored a touchdown on a five-yard (4.5-meter) run to help Ohio State win.

Of the 100 players who were in the game, 58 went on to play in the NFL (National Football League).

MOST VALUABLE PLAYER (OFFENSE):

CRAIG KRENZEL

MOST VALUABLE PLAYER (DEFENSE):

MIKE DOSS

2011 BCS National Championship

January 10, 2011

AUBURN TIGERS	22-19	OREGON DUCKS

UNIVERSITY OF PHOENIX STADIUM, GLENDALE, ARIZONA

The Tigers were led by stars Cam Newton and Michael Dyer. The Ducks were led by quarterback Darron Thomas and powerhouse running back LaMichael James.

In the second quarter, Auburn linebacker Mike Blanc tackled LaMichael James for a **safety**.

With two minutes left, the Ducks scored to tie the game. But in the final seconds, Tigers kicker Wes Byrum made a field goal for the win.

MOST VALUABLE PLAYER (OFFENSE):
MICHAEL DYER

MOST VALUABLE PLAYER (DEFENSE):
NICK FAIRLEY

2017 National Championship

January 9, 2017

CLEMSON TIGERS	35-31	ALABAMA CRIMSON TIDE

RAYMOND JAMES STADIUM, TAMPA, FLORIDA

Alabama scored two rushing touchdowns. By the fourth quarter, Alabama was ahead by three points with two minutes left in the game.

With one second left on the clock, Clemson quarterback Deshaun Watson threw to wide receiver Hunter Renfrow for the game-winning touchdown.

Clemson and Alabama have a long-standing **rivalry** that began when they first met on the field in 1900.

MOST VALUABLE PLAYER (OFFENSE):

DESHAUN WATSON

MOST VALUABLE PLAYER (DEFENSE):

BEN BOULWARE

2016 National Championship

January 11, 2016

ALABAMA CRIMSON TIDE 45-40 CLEMSON TIGERS

UNIVERSITY OF PHOENIX STADIUM, GLENDALE, ARIZONA

The fourth quarter was exciting with seven scoring plays. Alabama running back Kenyan Drake had a 95-yard (87-meter) kick return.

With one minute left in the game, Alabama was ahead 45 to 33.

In the final seconds, Clemson quarterback Deshaun Watson threw a 24-yard (22-meter) touchdown pass to tight end Jordan Leggett. It was not enough. Alabama won.

MOST VALUABLE PLAYER (OFFENSE):
O.J. HOWARD

MOST VALUABLE PLAYER (DEFENSE):
EDDIE JACKSON

2014 BCS National Championship

January 6, 2014

FLORIDA STATE SEMINOLES **34-31** AUBURN TIGERS

ROSE BOWL, PASADENA, CALIFORNIA

The Seminoles were led by star quarterback Jameis Winston. The Tigers had talented running back Tre Mason.

Florida State took the lead with a 100-yard (91-meter) **kickoff** return touchdown by Levonte Whitfield in the fourth quarter.

Auburn scored a touchdown with more than a minute left in the game. This gave the Seminoles one last chance. With 13 seconds on the clock, Jameis Winston threw a two-yard (1.8-meter) touchdown pass to Kelvin Benjamin for the win.

MOST VALUABLE PLAYER (OFFENSE):
JAMEIS WINSTON

MOST VALUABLE PLAYER (DEFENSE):
P.J. WILLIAMS

2018 National Championship

January 8, 2018

ALABAMA CRIMSON TIDE	26-23	GEORGIA BULLDOGS

MERCEDES-BENZ STADIUM, ATLANTA, GEORGIA

Georgia wide receiver Mecole Hardman made an 80-yard (73-meter) touchdown **reception** from quarterback Jake Fromm to lead by 13 points.

Alabama kicker Andy Pappanastos made two field goals to close the gap.

Then, Alabama tied the game with a touchdown reception thrown by quarterback Tua Tagovailoa. The game went into overtime.

Alabama wide receiver DeVonta Smith caught a 41-yard (37-meter) touchdown reception to get the win.

MOST VALUABLE PLAYER (OFFENSE):
TUA TAGOVAILOA

MOST VALUABLE PLAYER (DEFENSE):
DARON PAYNE

1998 Rose Bowl

January 1, 1998

MICHIGAN WOLVERINES 21-16 WASHINGTON STATE COUGARS

ROSE BOWL, PASADENA, CALIFORNIA

The Wolverines were undefeated. Washington State had not been to the Rose Bowl since 1931. Michigan had Heisman Trophy winner Charles Woodson. The Cougars were led by star quarterback Ryan Leaf.

In the fourth quarter, Michigan scored a touchdown. The Cougars had to settle for a field goal. The Wolverines led 21 to 16.

With two seconds left in the game, Ryan Leaf spiked the ball too late to stop the clock. The game was over.

MOST VALUABLE PLAYER:
BRIAN GRIESE

2006 Rose Bowl

January 4, 2006

TEXAS LONGHORNS	41-38	USC TROJANS

ROSE BOWL, PASADENA, CALIFORNIA

USC scored first with a touchdown in the first quarter. But Texas came back in the second quarter to score 16 points.

With seven minutes left in the game, USC was ahead by 12 points.

Texas quarterback Vince Young was able to close the gap with two touchdowns. A **two-point conversion** after the second touchdown assured a win for Texas.

MOST VALUABLE PLAYER (OFFENSE):

VINCE YOUNG

MOST VALUABLE PLAYER (DEFENSE):

MICHAEL HUFF

GLOSSARY

kickoff (KIK-awf): a kick of the ball that starts the action in a football game

overtime (OH-vur-time): extra time added to a game because the score was tied at the end of normal play

playoff (PLAY-awf): one of a series of games after the regular season that determine which teams will compete for the championship

reception (ri-SEP-shuhn): the catching of a forward pass by a receiver in football

rivalry (RYE-vuhl-ree): a long-standing competition between two teams

running back (RUN-ing bak): the player in football who carries the ball on running plays

safety (SAYF-tee): a football play in which a member of the offensive team is tackled behind its own goal line, earning two points for the defensive team

two-point conversion (too-poynt kuhn-VUR-zhuhn): a football play in which a team moves the football into the end zone to score two extra points after a touchdown

INDEX

AFTER READING QUESTIONS

1. Which game had the most players go into the NFL?
2. Which teams won their national championship games by only three points?
3. For how many years have Clemson and Alabama been rivals?
4. Who chooses which four teams will compete for a national championship?
5. What two teams played in the 1998 Rose Bowl?

About the Author

Ryan James lives in the western part of North Carolina with his dog Bailey. As a child growing up in South Florida, he became a huge fan of the Miami Hurricanes. When he is not watching college football games, he goes hiking and biking in the mountains near his home.

Written by: Ryan James
Cover Design by: Rhea Magaro-Wallace
Interior Design by: Kathy Walsh
Editor: Kim Thompson

Library of Congress PCN Data
Top College Football National Championship Games / Ryan James
Top Sports Championships
ISBN 978-1-63897-485-7 (hard cover)
ISBN 978-1-63897-600-4 (paperback)
ISBN 978-1-63897-715-5 (EPUB)
ISBN 978-1-63897-830-5 (eBook)
Library of Congress Control Number: 2022933973

Printed in the United States of America.

Photographs/Shutterstock: Cover ©winui, ©Justin Cooper; Title Pg ©winui, ©EFKS; Pg 3 ©EFKS; Pg 4, 6, 8, 10, 12, 14, 16, 18, 20 ©Sedulur Grafis; Pg 7, 9, 11, 13, 15, 17, 19, 21 ©Little_Monster_2070, Sakina Xalilova; Pg 5 ©Fred Kfoury III/Icon Sportswire; Pg 6 ©Walter G. Arce - AI Wire; Pg 8 ©Tony Leon; Pg 10 ©Scott Kelby; Pg 12 ©Charles Baus; Pg 14 ©Charles Baus; Pg 16 ©John Mersits; Pg 18 ©Jim Ruyman; Pg 20 ©Bahram Mark Sobhani

Seahorse Publishing Company
www.seahorsepub.com

Published in the United States
Seahorse Publishing
PO Box 771325
Coral Springs, FL 33077

SEAHORSE PUBLISHING